The Cozy Life

Rediscover the Joy of the
Simple Things Through the
Danish Concept of Hygge

Written & Illustrated by
Pia Edberg

ISBN: 1530746493
ISBN-13: 978-1530746491

www.piaedberg.com

Dedication

To my mother and father for always supporting me and providing me with a hyggeligt home.

And to my life partner, Tony Dean Smith, for his endless love and encouragement.

Table of contents

Acknowledgements

There were so many wonderful people who inspired me and kept me motivated to finish this book. Thank you for all of your support! I couldn't have done it without you.

To Chandler Bolt for providing me with the tools and resources to complete this book, to Diana Lim and Roy Yen for pushing me through my fears and keeping me on track with my goals, to my wonderful parents, Heini and Hortencia Edberg, for bringing me into this world and teaching me about the importance of family and a loving home, to my wonderful soul-mate and partner in crime, Tony Dean Smith, for always believing in me, and of course to my little fur-babies (cats), Charlie and Henry, for adding infinite amounts of *hygge* and love to my every day.

hygge (n/vb.): /HOO-gah/

the Danish concept of coziness...

...the art of creating warmth, comfort, and wellbeing through connection, treasuring the moment, and surrounding yourself with things you love.

A Special Note to the Reader

In today's world, we're constantly rushing from one thing to the next and struggling with information overload. When was the last time you took a moment to be still and ask yourself if you were happy?

Do you ever feel like you're just blindly grinding through the day, and when you finally do get a chance to pause, it's only to realize how much time has passed? Time is slipping through your hands, and the older you get, the faster it seems to fly.

Do you ever wish you had a better connection with yourself and those you care about? And what ever happened to the joy of simple things like a good conversation or a tasty, home-cooked meal?

This book is designed to help you slow down and enjoy life's cozy moments. It's about embracing the little things and getting back in touch with what's truly important.

I've devoted my life to self-improvement, devouring countless workshops, courses, and books, and through it all, I've found a simple solution to make life a million times sweeter. Whether you're learning about mindfulness or simplicity, finding your passion, or improving your relationships, adding a little *hygge* can make a whole world of difference.

What is *hygge*?

Hygge is a treasured cultural phenomenon among citizens of Denmark, which is consistently voted as one of the happiest countries in the world. Studies show that gratitude is often tied to overall wellbeing, and this book will show you the Danish way of achieving that connection through *hygge*.

I promise that if you take the time to read this short book and implement the concepts in your own life, you'll find yourself seeing the world with brand new eyes. You will feel more connected to yourself, the world, and the people all around you.

These pages hold the ingredients for creating a richer and deeper experience in everything we do. So if, perhaps, you want to wrap yourself in a lifestyle that feels like a warm hug, then this book is for you.

This transformation is meant to be easy and relaxed, just like *hygge*. And everyone is welcome. So find a comfortable place to read, grab your favourite hot beverage, light a candle, wrap yourself in a warm blanket or your coziest sweater, and *hygge* with me!

My Hygge Journey

It's the month of November in beautiful Vancouver, British Columbia, Canada. November here signifies the official transition from autumn to winter, and I can feel it in my bones. The leaves are turning shades of orange, red, and yellow as they cover the ground they fall upon. It's the perfect time to start writing a book about being warm and cozy! My "snowy pine and fir balsam" scented candle burns next to me, and I've got my comfiest slippers on my feet.

 Let's begin with my journey into the life-changing practice of *hygge*.

In the summer of 1984, I was born in Nykøbing Falster, just thirty minutes away from a tiny village called Hunseby on the Danish island of Lolland. My mother had moved to Denmark from the Philippines, and my father, a native Dane from Copenhagen, owned his own manufacturing company. He was born in the 1940s, so he was able to experience traditional *hygge,* before technology advanced Denmark into what it is today.

Christmastime was the quintessential season for us to *hygge*. Every year we chopped down our Christmas tree as a family and celebrated with *julefrokost*, a gathering of friends and family who ate a traditional meal of open-faced sandwiches and Aquavit, lasting for hours over candlelight. A wood-burning stove always kept the house warm and cozy in the wintertime. Summertime *hygge* consisted of meals out in the backyard, relaxing together under the sunset.

When I was five years old, we moved halfway across the world to Maple Ridge, British Columbia, a small suburb outside of Vancouver, Canada. I don't remember much, but I think I settled in fairly easily. I can't say it was the same for my parents, though.

Being immigrants, having to find their way and start from scratch must have been difficult. We didn't have a lot of money, and we lived in a tiny basement suite. But I loved it there and never felt the struggle. My father grew his business from the ground up, and my mother always made sure we had what we needed, whether it was a delicious, home-cooked meal or fresh sheets on our beds.

By the time I was nine, we had moved into a cute, little home in a small nearby heritage community called Hammond. Those were my favourite years as a child. I made the most incredible friends, and we'd spend the entire day playing outside and having adventures. *Hygge* came easily. It was truly about the joy in the simple things and surrounding myself with the ones I loved.

At fourteen I moved across town and had to change high schools. At the time, I was the awkward, lanky girl with braces who only ever wanted "peace on earth," and that didn't go over well with my new peers. These girls would call me names, spit on me, smear butter in my hair, and threaten to beat me up. My confidence plummeted. Things improved as we matured, but those memories stayed with me.

My early 20s were all about hedonism and seeking approval from others, probably because I was so scarred from high school and wanted so badly to fit in. I completed a University degree in Social Psychology and dabbled in song writing and guitar.

I ended up working in human resources (HR) for some amazing animation and film studios. HR seemed like an appropriate career, as I loved personal development and began reading stacks of self-help books. Looking back, I think I was craving to be understood, and I took it upon myself to make sure I understood others as well.

Then I had a bit of an early mid-life crisis. My long-term relationship fell apart. We had been living together for three years when we realized that we were not a good match for each other, and we began living completely separate lives.

Then I lost my job. I had to shut down a film studio and help my fellow colleagues deal with the emotional fallout. To top it off, I got involved in a new relationship that quickly turned toxic. My heart couldn't take it anymore. Somewhere along the way I went from being a confident and vibrant kid to being an insecure and confused young adult. I had lost who I was.

I did a great deal of soul searching and finally realized that nothing on the outside could make me happy. I had to find it on the inside. That's when I found minimalism.

I purged over half of my belongings, moved into a 500-square-foot studio apartment, and felt a new sense of freedom because I no longer had to worry about finances, spending too much time cleaning, and feeling the pressure to uphold an image dictated by society's standards. I was able to focus on what I really wanted and live life *my* way. I was actually happier with less stuff!

This type of *minimalism* is all about getting rid of excess distractions, whether it's the physical "stuff" we own, people we surround ourselves with, or unhealthy habits. By eliminating these distractions and simplifying our lives, we are able to think more clearly, be less stressed, and have more time to focus on the things that really matter to us, such as spending time with our loved ones, creativity, dreams, health, travel, and giving back.

While I embraced my new minimalist way of living, there was always something missing. It was a certain kind of warmth and coziness that was a familiar and intimate part of who I was. Getting rid of everything I owned only to have an empty apartment just wasn't cutting it. I didn't feel at home. I was missing *hygge*.

Hygge is about enjoying life's simple, cozy moments. It's like the minimalist concept, just taken up a notch. Life will always have its ups and downs, but I can confidently say that, now that I've reconnected with *hygge*, I'm moving towards living a more authentic and meaningful existence. I hope this book will inspire anyone who might be going through something similar.

In the following chapters, you'll learn about how you can add some of that magic to your own life. This book is divided into four sections; what *hygge* is, *hygge* foundations, the *hygge* lifestyle, and how *hygge* impacts your wellbeing.

But first, we must learn what this cozy concept is all about and where it came from.

My father (left), me (middle), and my mother (right). Denmark, 1985.

PART 1:
What Is Hygge?

What Is Hygge?

Hygge, pronounced HOO-gah, is both a noun and a verb and does not have a direct translation into English. The closest word would have to be *coziness,* but that doesn't really do it justice.

 While *hygge* is centered around cozy activities, it also includes a mental state of wellbeing and togetherness. It's a holistic approach to deliberately creating intimacy, connection, and warmth with ourselves and those around us.

When we *hygge,* we make a conscious decision to find joy in the simple things. For example, lighting candles and drinking wine with a close friend you haven't seen in a while, or sprawling out on a blanket while having a relaxing picnic in the park with a circle of your loved ones in the summertime are both *hygge.*

Though *hygge* is often a planned affair, it can be as simple as curling up and reading a good book on the sofa. It's about surrounding ourselves with everything we love and treasuring the moment. In a big departure from modern culture, we intentionally enjoy the domestic and personal aspects of life, rather than rushing through them just to make it through the day's tasks. We seek and embrace that warm, fuzzy feeling inside.

Danish researcher, Jeppe Trolle Linnet, even suggests that translating *hygge* into *homeyness* is more appropriate because in Scandinavia, the home is the one place where we can be ourselves and shut out negativity from the world outside. It's so important to have a place where we can go and feel protected from it all; it's something we all deserve.

While *hygge* is typically associated with the colder seasons of fall and winter, you can *hygge* in the spring and summertime as well. Picnics in the park, lazy beach days, music festivals, barbecues, and bicycle rides are all *hygge*. There's nothing better than spending the day at the beach with friends and having no other plans scheduled.

When we can enjoy what is right in front of us, we end up living a life that is truly present.

With *Hygge* we create a safe haven where we can relax without pressures to be anyone else but who we are. We invite those we love into our world and create an environment of togetherness.

"Hygge is where the heart and the soul meet."

Hygge History & Danish Roots

 *Hygge's* roots originate in Denmark, a Scandinavian country in Northern Europe located just southwest of Sweden. Even though, when winter rolls around, Denmark has over 17 hours of darkness per day and an average temperature of 0 degrees Celsius, it has still been ranked the happiest country in the world according to the United Nations World Happiness Report in 2013 and 2014 and was third in 2015. Researchers looked at factors, such as work-life balance (a regular work week is 37 hours plus at least five weeks of vacation per year), generous parental leave, high-quality healthcare, gender equality, unemployment benefits, security of employment, political freedom, low crime, and an uncorrupted government.

Denmark consistently ranks well despite having some of the highest taxes in the report, which goes to show that *hygge* and happiness are not about money at all. *Hygge* is about enjoying the simple things, rather than accumulating material possessions. A sense of community and enjoying time spent with your loved ones is more important. The Danes take their leisure time seriously and know the art of *hygge* well.

The Danish respect for the simple things is related to the concept of *Janteloven* (jante-law), which states that you are no better than anyone else. I can see how it can be both despised and respected in Denmark, like being pulled in two opposite directions.

On one hand, individuality allows us to express our unique, colourful personalities and strive for our own successes. On the other hand, *Janteloven* allows for more of an equality-based society because competition is not necessary, and everyone is treated the same. You won't be judged by what you choose to do for a living. As long as you are happy, that's all that matters. Because of this, there is less disappointment and more satisfaction with life.

The word *hygge* originates from the 18th Century and an Old Norse concept of wellbeing. Jeppe Trolle Linnet describes it as a "safe habitat; the experience of comfort and joy, especially in one's home and family; a caring orientation, for example, toward children; a civilized mode of behaviour that other people find easy to get along with, one that soothes them and builds their trust; a house that, while not splendid or overly stylish, is respectably clean and well-kept." *Hygge* is a classless concept, inviting all to participate.

There are similar concepts to *hygge* in a few other countries:

- *Wabi-sabi* from Japan is the idea of finding the beauty in things that are imperfect.

- *Friluftsliv* from Norway translates to "open-air life." This is about living a life of enjoying nature.

- *Gemütlichkeit* from Germany is akin to *hygge*.

- *Gezelligheid* from Holland is also much like *hygge*.

As you can imagine, because Danish winters are so long and dark, the Danes needed to find a way to enjoy this time of the year without going mad. That's when all the candles come out and people *hygge*. Christmas is when Danes go all out with *hygge*. You will see lights, candles, greenery, and traditional Christmas decorations all over people's homes, in the shops, in the pubs, and even at Tivoli Gardens, Denmark's famous amusement park that attracts thousands of visitors from all over the world.

Hygge Stories

My father is now 75 years old, and since he was able to experience Denmark before technology took over, I wanted to add his concept of *hygge* to our discussion. I think it's really beautiful to see the perspective of someone who had lived in a simpler time.

What's your definition of Hygge?

> *There are a lot of things that have to add up. You need togetherness, with family, friends, and neighbours, candlelights, and the smell of wood smoke from a wood stove. You start to feel good; it's a matter of liking it, and you are together with people you like. Hygge is old-fashioned and informal.*

Where did Hygge come from?

> *Denmark is small country. There were small farms and you lived close to your neighbours. People always needed each other once in a while. Kids would play with neighbours, and the neighbours' kids would come over.*

Sooner or later, the parents eventually met each other. In the countryside they'd help each other during the harvest time. Also, if someone was ill, they'd help each other, like taking care of the kids if the mom was ill. They had close relationships to their neighbours.

In the old days there was no electricity, no TV, no entertainment, and no Internet. So what they did was at home they used candlelight. Candles were quite expensive—everyone was poor in these days—so they had to save money to buy candles.

When it got cold, everybody would gather in the kitchen because that's where the cast-iron stove was for cooking. It was too expensive to heat the whole house up. But they were never idling. They were always busy.

They would sit with candles while knitting. Families would tell stories of their youth and everything they experienced in their lives. They'd be having small snacks, like baked apples with sugar and cinnamon if it was fancy. And it tasted damn good.

It was common for people to pick elderberries, warm them up with sugar and spices, like cinnamon, and sit there drinking that stuff.

 *As time passed by, and depending if it was a richer family, they might make Jule Gløgg (mulled wine) where they warm up red wine, put raisins in, split almonds, some beer, hard liquor and sugar; it's a sweet drink. They'd bake some cookies with cinnamon, too.*

What makes things Hygge?

It starts with being cold outside. Maybe you were out having a long walk or whatever. You come inside in the kitchen where everything takes place. And somebody at home had been making all the food. You can smell it. There are nice decorations and candlelight.

You come in in the warmth, and you feel good. Everybody is in a good mood, joking and smiling and telling stories. Nothing expensive is served; it's all plain and simple, home-baked cookies. You can't experience hygge if you talk about TV, Internet and cellphones. Those are totally opposite of hygge and having a good time together.

You don't see hygge in North America because people haven't experienced this kind of togetherness. In Denmark, they have a saying around Christmastime: if someone comes to your house in the middle of the winter, you always have to give them a small treat, because you can't take Christmas away from anyone.

You would invite the postman inside for a cup of coffee because he was part of the society. He'd provide messages from house to house and knew what was going on.

When you've grown up with hygge, it comes as a natural thing. In old days, at the end of November when Christmas was coming, everyone was busy. The mom would be home together with the kids making Christmas decorations and baking cookies.

How do people Hygge today?

Well they sort of do it the same way, but people in the modern world are always on an electronic device. What counts is the relationship.

It's really about simplicity, and it also goes for the food. Food is simple and homemade. You eat the old-fashioned stuff that has been made for generations.

Do you have any favourite Hygge stories?

We had just moved to Hunseby from Lolland and had a horse that needed hay. We couldn't find hay, but someone told us there was a small castle where they probably had some. So we phoned them, and they said we could stop by. It was getting dark, and it was frosty, but we got a few bales of hay.

Then they invited us into their kitchen, and it was a really nice sight—a big country kitchen and a huge, cast-iron stove where they were preparing food. All over the ceiling were a lot of red hearts cut out of cardboard, hanging from wooden beams. They made the hot Swedish punch, Jule Gløgg.

There were a few people there, and when we came in we were greeted, "Hi, how are you?" It was a very warm welcome even though they've never seen us before. We got some food, and it was really nice coming from the cold to some friendly people. The whole environment was very cozy. I remember this story because it was with strangers.

Do you have any final thoughts?

If I try to analyze what makes the difference, it comes from the fact that

Denmark is such a small country, and in Denmark people don't move around every two years. People stay in the same place their whole lives and learn about the people around them. Here in Canada people moved around every year to flip their house and make some money so you never learn the name of your neighbour.

Tradition is very important, like when I have my annual Christmas lunch. Hygge is old fashioned. There was no entertainment in the old days. Someone would sit reading stories, talking about old times, and inventing their own entertainment, like making homemade dolls. The men would usually sit around and make baskets out of willow trees. This was to hold the firewood.

It's really a time you appreciate. It's valuable time socially, and you get good food and drink. You'll remember when you've had these good times.

My father always brings such a unique perspective to things. He sees the world vividly and remembers every detail no matter how long ago the event was.

The more I learn about *hygge*, the more important I feel it is to experience it. Life can pass us by so quickly, and before we know it, it's gone. All those small moments in between the big moments are just as important and precious. Feelings of connection, presence, simplicity, and joy are what enriches our lives at a deeper level.

"There's no place like home."
~ Dorothy, The Wizard of Oz

PART 2:
Hygge Foundations

Hygge Foundations

So, how do we *hygge?* What are the foundations of *hygge?* For some of us, creating a *hyggeligt* (*hygge*-like) atmosphere comes naturally, as it's something we're already drawn to. Maybe you already enjoy a relaxed lifestyle and surround yourself with things you love. For me, it has always meant feeling comfort and a sense of belonging, no matter what kind of situation I was in.

It could have been during school, at work, or with a new group of people I've never met. There's a certain kind of energy that fills the space, and you either feel like you belong there or you don't.

Hygge is a very personal and individual thing, and what makes you happy compared to someone else isn't always the same. The goal however, is to feel like you're at "home"—safe, happy, connected, and present.

Hygge is as much an internal (emotional/psychological) phenomenon as it is external (in the way we behave and the things that we do).

I found that there were some common themes that made a situation *hygge,* such as how it feels, valuing simplicity, slowing down, the atmosphere, the company, how we host, the mindset, generosity, and the importance of authenticity. These all lead to enjoying life just a little bit more and making it richer and deeper.

What Does Hygge Feel Like?

Close your eyes for a moment, and think about a time in your life when you were a child and felt safe, relaxed, and completely free to be yourself. Who were you with? Your mother? Your father? A grandparent or sibling? Maybe you were even by yourself.

What were you doing? Drawing a picture? Helping your father bake your favourite cookies? Lying on a rooftop and gazing at the stars or watching your favourite sports team on the television with your family? Maybe you were cuddling in your mother's arms or holding your older sister's hand as she walked you to the park.

What were the qualities of that moment?

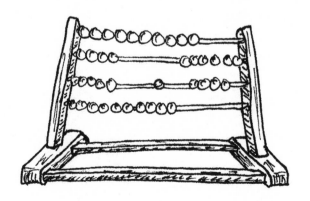

Some of my favourite calming moments as a child were when my mother, my father, and I would go on long drives to run errands in another town. There was something so soothing about sitting in a vehicle for hours, taking in the scenery while deep in my thoughts and safe in my parents' company.

I felt like nothing bad could happen to me as long as I had them by my side. It seems so simple, but it was precious to me. It's still one of my favourite things to do to this day— running boring errands with anyone who will have me for company.

It will be slightly different for everyone, as we all have our experiences and things that comfort us, but that's perhaps how *hygge* might feel. *Hygge* is a safe haven protecting you from anything bad *out there*, and surrounding yourself with things you love. It has a nostalgic quality to it.

Another example would be the way you feel during Christmas or Thanksgiving when you are surrounded by loved ones, good food, and a cozy atmosphere. The only difference is that *hygge* is applied to your life all year round!

Anything can be made to feel cozy and at any time.

"Hygge was never meant to be translated—it was meant to be felt."
~ ToveMaren Stakkestad

Jot down some favourite childhood memories.

_____

_____

_____

_____

_____

_____

_____

_____

_____

Simplicity

Hygge is a simple concept, and it's all about appreciating the little things in life. The Danes tend to be a lot less materialistic than other cultures. This is because they value experiences and connecting with friends and family, over accumulating vast amounts of stuff. The best things in life are free, and the most memorable activities can cost little to nothing, such as a picnic in a park or watching the snow fall with a cup of hot chocolate and a good friend. If everyone adopted a little more *hygge* in their lives, we'd have happier, more relaxed people and a more caring world.

Slowing Down

We live in a culture full of distractions, and because of this, we suffer from information overload. Our daily lives are rushed as everything competes for our attention, and we rarely take the time out of our days to be still. Sometimes, we can get so wrapped up in our to-do lists we forget to pause, slow down, and relax.

Slowing down is key to experiencing *hygge* because it lets us connect with ourselves again. Turn off all of the technology! When the candles are lit, put your phones and other electronic devices away. Slowing down takes practice and may be uncomfortable at first, but it's in those silent moments that we get to rebalance, recharge, and reconnect. Go ahead and try it. Take the next 20 minutes to just be with yourself.

> *"Slow down; there is more to life*
> *than simply increasing its speed."*
> *~ Mahatma Gandhi*

The Hyggeligt Atmosphere

The *hyggeligt* atmosphere exudes warmth and coziness. It is safe, easygoing, and laidback, and there is no competition. It's about having fun, but not like when you're at a raging party. It's more relaxed and intimate. You feel content and pleased. Your thoughts are not here, nor there, and you aren't worrying about that *thing* you need to get done the next day. There is no need to rush.

Conversation can be deep or light, and often times jokes or stories are told. *Hygge* is not about having heated debates about politics or religion. It's valuable time you spend with your loved ones in a peaceful and calming environment.

> *"Hygge as practiced by Danes has special characteristics. First, it depends on the complete and positive participation of all present in the encounter... Second, it requires an evenness of flow, a sustained back-and-forth dance of involvement that encourages and even demands this level of participation. And third, the*

achievement of these goals is made possible by a range of positive social skills, including teasing (a national pastime), quick repartee, the telling of stories and jokes, patience, sensitivity, and the ability to be an enthusiastic audience as well as performer. The ability to participate easily in social encounters that bring this principle to life is a part of the Danish heritage that others can well regard with envy." – Stephen Borish in his ethnography of Danish sociality quoted in Jeppe Trolle Linnet in Money Can't Buy Me Hygge.

Hygge does not always need to involve other people. We can *hygge* just as well when we're alone, and we can bring *hygge* into everything we do in our daily lives, such as our morning routine or the way we make dinner. And that's the beauty of it. H*ygge* is available and accessible to everyone no matter who you are or where you come from. *Hygge* can be spontaneous or planned; there are no rules!

"Hygge is in everything we want it to be in."

Hygge Company

The best people to *hygge* with are those you enjoy being around the most. It could be with good friends, family, your partner, your neighbour, colleagues from work, or even just your own company. But it's important that you are with people that make you feel safe and comfortable to be who you are.

It sounds a bit cheesy, but one of my favourite things to do is to sit in a circle on the floor with my dearest friends, dim the lights, pour a glass of wine, and just talk about life. I could do that for days!

And who says *hygge* has to be limited to people? Pets are the perfect *hygge* companions! I know my two fluffy cats, Charlie and Henry, make the best cozy company.

> *"No road is long with good*
> *company."*
> *~ Turkish Proverb*

Hygge Company: me with my two cats, Charlie (left) and Henry (right).

Authenticity

Authenticity is a word that gets thrown around a lot, but what does it really mean?

When you break it down, authenticity is the quality of being real. Genuine. Down to earth. I see it in relation to the idea of being your true self, following your bliss, living according to your values, and connecting with your pure essence or spirit no matter what the outside world tells you.

Authenticity requires self-awareness. Once we know who we are, we can properly pursue a happy and fulfilled life, whether it's in our careers, relationships, hobbies, or goals. Take a moment in your day to write down your thoughts and feelings about things that you love and value. Write about what you are and aren't drawn to. Listen to your intuition, and trust your inner dialogue. The journey to finding our inner voice is something we all go through, and as we grow and evolve, our personalities grow and evolve with us. Take the time to reflect; we learn and discover new things about ourselves every day.

In the context of *hygge,* being completely authentic is essential. There should be no pretending or putting on a false image. As soon as we start to worry about how to act or what to wear, we lose the *hyggeligt* feeling. It's about having an open heart, being kind to others, and being easy on ourselves.

There is no need to seek approval or impress anyone. Sometimes, in North American culture, we feel the need to prove how successful or interesting we are to everyone else. But this is not the case for *hygge.* When you *hygge,* you indulge in the moment without worrying about being anyone else but yourself. You're carefree and at ease, accepting and accepted for who you are, not the things you have.

Remember, you can't make everyone like you. If you pretend to be someone else, you will attract the wrong people. If you choose to be yourself, you'll attract the right people and they will be

your people.

A *hyggeligt* environment is peaceful, and that includes a safe place for our emotional wellbeing. *Hygge* is to shut out the external world and wrap ourselves in a safe and magical environment with those we want to spend our time with. Nothing should be forced, and the moment should unfold naturally and comfortably.

So talk about topics that interest you. Talk about your biggest dreams or how nice it is to be there with your friends. Or if you prefer, simply don't feel the need to speak at all, and just enjoy the silence.

> *"Only the truth of who you are, if realized, will set you free."*
> *~ Eckhart Tolle*

Take a moment to write down the things you value the most.

_____

_____

_____

Adopting the Hygge Mindset

The *hygge* mindset is about looking on the bright side of things and having a positive outlook even when the situation seems lousy.

I've lost my job before, just like anyone else. The first time was stressful. I was overwhelmed, and I didn't know what to do. But when it happened again, I learned that it was a blessing in disguise. As one door closed, another opened up, and the new opportunity led me closer to what I wanted. I learned that dealing with "negative" events is all about perspective.

Hygge is about embracing the situation no matter how bad we perceive it to be. For instance, think about those times when the weather outside was miserable—dark, rainy and freezing cold. But with *hygge* we LOVE days like this. Yes! It's the perfect opportunity to put on our warmest, comfiest pyjamas, curl up in a blanket, and watch a movie.

It's normal for us to complain when the weather gets a little gloomy. I can especially relate, as Vancouver is also known as *Raincouver*. But try to find something to love about the "bad" weather. Put on your favourite jacket, woolly scarf, and toque, and go for a walk to take in the beauty of nature. Or build a snowman in the newly fallen snow.

Anytime you find yourself complaining, think of ways to try to flip the negative in your mind into a positive. As the old saying goes:

> *"There's no such thing as bad*
> *weather, only bad clothes."*
> *~ Norwegian proverb*

Generosity

Hygge is kind, generous, and giving. We give *hygge* to our friends and family when we invite them over for dinner, and we give *hygge* to ourselves to nourish our souls.

If we have children, we teach them how to appreciate the simple things. We encourage them to try things for themselves and include them in everyday tasks, teaching them that doing the dishes or helping out with dinner are not annoying chores, but are essential activities to making daily life more joyful.

It's important to understand the emotional and psychological foundations of *hygge* before embarking on such everyday, practical things. Take the time to dig deep, slow down, and pay attention to the world around you. You might see something you've never noticed before.

Coming up, you'll learn to integrate some super cozy activities into your daily life. You may already be doing some of these things, but with *hygge* we kick them up a notch!

magical

coziness warmth

homeyness comfort summer **simplicity**

friendship kinfolk intimacy connection

safe vanilla family **peaceful** joy calming **happiness**

trust candlelight food cookies tea blankets spring

scarves wine security autumn familiarity **hygge**

reassurance pine trees **informal** sincere down to earth close

convivial **relaxed** comfortable plaid

winter **snug** friendly welcoming unwind **authenticity**

tranquil atmosphere egalitarian wellbeing home

hyggeligt childhood reassurance

cinnamon living well

PART 3:
The Hygge Lifestyle

Hygge Is Everywhere

Hygge is everywhere. Or should I say, it *can* be everywhere if we want it to be. Let's look at some of the more practical ways we can incorporate *hygge* into our daily lives, whether it's in creating a cozy home, baking traditional Danish desserts, or *hyggeligt* ways to spend time with our loved ones. Hopefully you'll walk away with a taste of how *hygge* can be applied to any area of your life.

When I think about *hygge,* I imagine an old-fashioned sort of life: simple, nostalgic, self-sufficient, community oriented, spending quality time with our loved ones, putting technology away, and appreciating the outdoors.

Here are some ways to add some magic to the everyday!

The Hyggeligt Home

Whenever I'm at home, I want to feel so incredibly comfortable and cozy that I never want to leave. When I curl up on the sofa, I want pillows and blankets to be available, and textures to be soft. And when I enjoy a glass of red wine, I want to light a candle and really take the time to savor my drink.

Whether you're in the process of setting up or revamping your home, we can choose to be more mindful and pay attention to how we want everything to be. Some of us love decorating our space down to the tiniest detail, while some of us have other interests and don't want to put much energy into it. But the important thing is that you are happy and that you surround yourself with things that you love.

It's easy to start small, even on a tight budget. Scented candles are a great addition, and they won't break the bank. Try anything natural or homey, like pine, vanilla, or spice. I especially like scents that remind me of baked goods. These aromas will calm your soul, and the light will give the room a warm, gentle, *hyggeligt* glow.

If you live with other people, whether they're family or roommates, see if you can involve them and get them excited about it. But even if your only options are your bedroom or other personal spaces, you'll still have a good start.

Either way, once people see how much of an impact your *hygge* lifestyle has on you and how it improves your life, they will surely follow suit. Don't be afraid to speak to your partner about how important this is to you. Happiness and harmony are necessary, after all.

While we can technically *hygge* anywhere, we most often do so at home. Your home should have a general sense of tidiness, but it doesn't need to be so pristine that it feels clinical and cold. Too much chaos isn't good, either. It's about striking the perfect balance: lived in, but organized. It should feel comfortable.

Be mindful of you and your family when designing your interior space. Don't be a hoarder, and don't buy things just because they're on sale. Decorate with purpose, and remove any excess clutter that no longer serves a function. Don't forget that one (wo)man's trash, is another (wo)man's treasure. Donate your old items to your local thrift shop or charity so that someone else can enjoy your previously loved things.

With that said, it's OK to hold onto sentimental items or heirlooms. But be choosy; you don't want to be so emotionally attached to your belongings that you can't part with anything.

Sentimental items remind us that we have a history, and they tell a deeper story about who we are and where we come from. They trigger all sorts of warm feelings when they remind us of another time, place, or person. *Hygge* is old fashioned; there is a nostalgic, magical quality to it, and our homes are a reflection of who we are and what we love. I love surrounding myself with things that each tell a story.

Choose a home that feels inviting when you walk in. You can feel that it is the right place for you. Usually it's because there is a familiar quality to it that brings us to a place of safety and comfort. I've always preferred older, heritage homes, as it's what I grew up with; Denmark has plenty of houses that are well over 400 years old. And though I didn't grow up in a home of luxury, my family was always able to make our space beautiful in simple and inexpensive ways.

Lastly, don't be too caught up with perfection. It's well-known that Danes put a lot of thought into design and spaces, but it's really about choosing and caring for the few things that you love—quality over quantity.

Be happy with what you have. A *hyggeligt* home is welcoming, cozy, and inviting and reflects the personality of the owner.

"Surround yourself with things that you love."

Home Décor

When creating a *hyggeligt* home, it's important not to take décor too seriously. You want to express yourself and create a feeling of homeyness, so it should come naturally. Pay less attention to your head and more attention to your heart. Listen to your intuition. Take a look at your current surroundings, and see if you want to edit anything.

Don't worry about the latest design trends or what someone else might think of your choices. Trust in your own opinion, even if at first glance things don't seem to really go together.

Take these elements into consideration when setting out to create a *hyggeligt* home:

Textures

Decorate your home with soft textures, such as knitted or fleece throw blankets, fluffy pillows, shag rugs, and comfortable furniture. The idea here is that no matter where you sit or stand, it feels pleasant against your skin.

Lighting

Lighting is another key element and should be very calming and therapeutic. There's a noticeable difference between white, fluorescent lights overhead and the warm, yellow glow from a table lamp. One light is more inviting than the other.

If you want light overhead, try stringing up some faery lights. The idea is to have warm lighting that mimics the natural glow of fire. And if you have a fireplace or candles, use them! They aren't just decorative; they're *hyggeligt*.

Bring in the Outdoors

Since, genetically speaking, we are animals, we are instinctively drawn to nature. So how about bringing the outside in? Plants offer excellent health benefits, from bringing us oxygen, cleaning the air, and boosting our mental wellbeing.

You can pick up small plants for as little as $1.99 from your local nursery. Surrounding yourself with greenery will add peace and *hygge* to any home. Try hanging plants from the ceiling or building your own terrarium.

Additionally, decorate with materials that are natural and of the earth, such as metals, wood, stone, and leather. This could be reclaimed wooden furniture, antique metal candleholders, or even rock collections. The goal is to remind us of nature even when we're indoors.

Pets

Why stop at plants as your only source of nature? Pets can be equally as calming. There's nothing more peaceful than having a napping cat in your lap, a dog at your feet, or fish swimming around in an aquarium.

Colour

When choosing colours for paint or décor, go for warmer tones. There are cool and warm versions of colours, and being mindful of which you choose will impact the energy of the room. If it interests you, learn about colour psychology and how colour affects your mood.

Furniture

Furniture should look inviting. You should want to curl up in it and enjoy a good book. Choose furniture that has rounded edges versus straight, solid lines. And always try before you buy! Nothing is worse than bringing a new sofa home only to discover that it's hard as a rock. (I've made that mistake!)

Embrace the Unexpected

A *hyggeligt* home is slightly eclectic. The degree of that is up to you, of course, but don't be afraid to mix and match items! For instance, rich velvet upholstery and faux fur rugs layered on top of low pile rugs. Mix and match the old and the new, the modern and the antique.

Express Yourself

Lastly, don't forget to express your quirky, whimsical side. That weird statue you found at a flea market? Put it near the door so people see it when they walk in. And that funny movie poster?

That can go in the bathroom. Again, it's all about surrounding yourself with things that you love. This is where you belong, after all. So display your antique book collection, and hang photos of your family where you'll notice them every day.

Hosting the Hygge Way

Before I started learning about *hygge*, I never put too much thought into the art of hosting. I figured as long as my guests had something to drink and were comfortable, they were fine. But there's more to it than that. Here are a few things that can help you host your next event the *hygge* way:

- When your guests have arrived, be sure to ask them if they want something to eat or to drink. It shows your manners in a warm and caring way. Be generous, open, and giving.

- Your home doesn't need to be spotless in order to have guests over. There can be pressure for some of us to only invite anyone over when the house is in impeccable condition, but there is no need for that.

- Tables are usually set with several candles and a centerpiece of greenery.

- Simplicity is key to hosting the *hygge* way. A plate of freshly baked cookies and some tea, or a cheese plate, grapes, and a glass of wine will do just fine.

- If guests offer to help, be okay with that. Working together and helping one another creates a *hyggeligt* environment. *Hygge* is about teamwork and everyone participating. Potlucks are great for this.

- Always have a few bottles of wine and some snacks stocked up to offer any surprise guests who show up.

- When it comes to the sitting area, there shouldn't be too much empty space around people. Smaller, intimate spaces are more *hyggeligt*.

- Lighting candles creates a relaxing mood instantly.

- Be easygoing, calm down, and unwind. Be comfortable sitting in silence if the moment calls for it. Feel free to let time stand still with no worries. Have deep conversations, and enjoy the moment. Linger.

Unexpected Guests

There have been numerous times when a guest would randomly show up and I'd frantically have to tidy up the house, hoping it looked somewhat presentable. If we want to have people over more often, we can't get too stressed out about making sure our home is spotless. The most effective way to quickly tidy up is to focus on the areas that people will actually be spending their time in. Close the doors to any rooms that will not be used.

Then follow these six simple steps, and be on your way to *hygge* hosting heaven!

Step 1: Don't stress about perfection.

Step 2: Vacuum or sweep the floors.

Step 3: Wipe down tabletops.

Step 4: Put items away that don't belong.

Step 5: Clean glass and mirrors.

Step 6: Light candles! They cover up any unwanted smells, and they give the room an inviting, hyggeligt glow.

Doing Chores

Most people don't enjoy doing chores. Sure, there's a handful who get excited about cleaning toilets, but for the rest of us, adding some *hygge* can help:

- Listen to music, dance, and sing along. This can make chores a lot more fun.

- Make your bed every morning. It sets the tone for the day.

- Open the windows and let in the fresh air.

- Time yourself to see if the task really takes as long as you think it does. You'd be surprised.

- Be present and mindful when doing chores. Gain awareness of every touch, smell, and movement.

- Make chores into a fun game. Reward yourself at the end.

- Take breaks.

- Get help. *Hygge* is communal, so if you can, recruit other family members.

- Simplify and declutter your home. Get rid of excess junk that is no longer serving you.

Hygge at Work

Though work and *hygge* technically contradict one another, there are ways to incorporate some of that coziness into the workplace. A *hyggeligt* company values friendliness, trust, and teamwork, and a flat hierarchical structure usually supports this.

Some of us work in offices or cubicles and spend eight or more hours there each day. It only makes sense that our office space should feel more *hyggeligt* by adding some personal touches and calming elements to boost our happiness and focus.

In my office at work I've tried to incorporate some *hygge* by adding a comfortable chair, some faery lights, my guitar, plants, and nature-inspired artwork made out of painted wood. Not only do I feel more relaxed when I'm working, but I always receive compliments on having the most inviting office.

Keeping in mind what we've learned about the *hyggeligt* home, here are some ways that you can make your workspace more comfortable:

Lighting

Find a cozy table lamp, or add faery lights.

Personal Items

Add something personal that reflects who you are or reminds you of something you love. Family photos can especially add a sense of homeyness.

Inspiring Quotes

Decorate your space with inspiring words to motivate you.

Fun Stationery

Choose office supplies that are fun and creative.

Colours

Decorate your space with your favourite warm colours.

Plants

Add plants. Studies have shown that plants help us improve concentration, memory, and productivity. They also have a calming effect on the soul.

Comfy Furniture

Having the right kind of furniture, especially a nice, comfy chair, makes your space more inviting.

Artwork

Choose art that calms you and brings you joy.

Textures

If you have the space, adding rugs and pillows can greatly increase the *hyggeness* of your office.

Hyggeligt Attire

Hyggeligt attire is anything that you feel comfortable in. Think plaid patterns, big woolly sweaters, leggings, scarves, toques, flannel shirts, plush socks, and cozy winter boots. Don't forget some big fluffy slippers!

Clothing tends to be casual. There's no need to fuss over how you look. Life isn't a fashion show, after all. Nobody cares about that when you're having a good time. If you feel like you have to be too stylish, you're feeling the need to pretend. Don't pretend. You have to feel at home. If you don't feel at home, then it's not *hygge*.

Hygge Music

Music can be *hyggeligt*, too! *Hyggeligt* music is anything that soothes the soul and calms the mind. It is nothing too exciting or loud. Sometimes *hyggeligt* music can have a melancholy quality, but it is usually pleasant and takes you to another place.

Classical music is a good choice or some Ray Lamontagne, Bon Iver, Mree, James Morrison, Damien Rice, or Lana Del Rey if you're into indie sounds. Personally, I love playing classic hits from the '50s to '90s, as they trigger a nostalgic feeling for me.

Hygge Scents

It's easy to overlook the impact that smells have on us, but science says that scents are strongly linked to memories. If we smell something familiar, we will have vivid recollections of another time and place long forgotten.

There are smells I typically associate with *hygge,* such as a homemade meal, cinnamon buns, vanilla, and pumpkin. However, we don't always have time to be baking 24 hours a day, so why not incorporate scented candles that smell like freshly baked cookies, pine trees, or burning firewood?

You can also pick up an essential oil diffuser at an aromatherapy shop. They'll usually have hundreds of fragrances to choose from, so you'll be able to find your own personal *hygge*. If you're into something a little more new-age, Nag Champa incense sticks are always a classic. Or, if you want to keep it simple, just place a few pinecones in a bowl on the dining room table for a wintery aroma.

In Denmark, we would make Pomanders—the tradition of piercing cloves into oranges, which would draw out the citrus and spicy aromas. Pomanders were historically used to mask odours during Victorian times. Try it for yourself!

Pomander Instructions

You'll need: oranges, cloves

Stick the pointy long end of the cloves into the orange in any design you prefer. Place them in a bowl, and voila! They smell absolutely heavenly. Or, if you'd like, try tying a ribbon or string around them, and hang them up.

Tea vs. Coffee

While tea and coffee are both warm and soothing, I find that they represent different motivations and purposes. Drinking tea reminds me of slowing down my body, mind, and soul. It symbolizes an afternoon break or is part of an evening bedtime ritual.

Coffee, on the other hand, is about speeding up, increasing energy to get you through the day with that quick caffeine hit. When I've had a late night and have to wake up for an early morning, a cup of coffee will give me that extra boost.

Both beverages are *hygge* in their own way. Sitting in a coffee shop with a hot latte is just as cozy as sipping on herbal tea before bedtime.

Whatever your beverage of choice is, creating simple rituals will make preparing tea or coffee that much more pleasant. Pick up a beautiful teapot or mug that appeals to you. Invest in high-quality coffee, or fancy blends of loose-leaf teas.

We can also incorporate the teachings of herbology, the study of plants for medicinal purposes. If you're lucky enough to live near a place that sells herbs, or you want to grow and dry them on your own, you can blend and brew them much like you would a tea. Below is my favourite blend that is a great remedy if you're suffering from nervousness, anxiety, or a busy mind. The plants' synergy amplifies each other's effects. At low doses this tea is relaxing. At high doses it can be sedating or even psychedelic due to the passionflower.

Peaceful Dream Tea

Ingredients: chamomile, lavender, cinnamon bark, passionflower, rose petals, and spearmint.

Directions: mix ingredients in equal parts, place one tablespoon into a loose leaf tea diffuser, and steep for at least 15 minutes. Enjoy!

Hygge Recipes

The Danes cherish anything homemade or that reminds them of childhood, and that goes for meals, desserts, and  treats. The more heart and history that goes into the creation of something, the more *hyggeligt* it is.

In that spirit, I'd like to share some of my favourite *hygge* foods that I enjoyed growing up with. They're all simple and easy-to-make Danish traditional recipes, and I know you will love them just as much as I do.

In order to add that extra spirit of *hygge,* try to bake with the *hyggeligt* frame of mind. Put love and attention into every detail. Play some relaxing music or wear your favourite apron. Smile. It will make your desserts taste that much sweeter. When you're finished, invite some friends over to enjoy the dishes with you!

Fruit Dessert
("Rødgrød med Fløde" – Jordbær Grød, Rabarber Grød, Hindbær Grød)

This dish is a classic Danish dessert, and you can eat it all year round. When I was a child I would have it smothered in cream. Strawberry was my favourite, but you can use any kind of berries that are in season.

2 lbs	**berries (strawberries, rhubarb, or raspberries)**
750 ml (3 cups)	**water**
150 ml (2/3 cup)	**sugar, to taste**
3-4 tbsp	**cornstarch**

Clean and rinse the berries, place in a pot with water, and bring to a boil. Remove from heat, stir in the sugar, and thicken with cornstarch dissolved in water. Return to a boil, stirring for 2-3 minutes until thickened. Pour into a serving bowl with light cream or milk. Serves 6.

Rice Pudding (Ris A L'amande)

Traditionally, ris a l'amande was eaten for dinner before the main meat course. Families would also leave a portion of the porridge in their barns for the elves to eat, which kept them happy. Because of urbanization, whipped cream, sugar, and chopped almonds were added to the recipe, and it was topped with a warm cherry sauce. If you find the whole almond, you win a marzipan pig with a red ribbon! My family and I make this once a year, for our Christmas Eve dessert, and I always eat several bowlfuls!

1L (4 cups)	**milk**
150 ml (2/3 cup)	**short-grained white rice**
1/2	**vanilla pod**
1/2 tsp	**salt**
200 ml (3/4 cup)	**almonds, blanched and chopped, 1 whole almond**
500 ml (2 cups)	**whipping cream**
2 tbsp	**sugar**
	cherry sauce

Bring milk, rice, and vanilla pod to a boil. Simmer over low heat for about 1 hour or until rice is done and milk has thickened, stirring occasionally. Add salt. Cool completely! Mix in almonds and sugar. Whip cream and fold into rice mixture. Refrigerate. Serve with warm cherry sauce. Serves 6.

Ebleskiver (Æbleskiver)

This is one of my favourite treats. Ebleskiver are similar to donut holes made out of delicious, fluffy pancake batter with a lemony, spicy twist. You can eat them for breakfast or for a snack. But I bet you can't eat just one!

875 ml (3.5 cups)	flour
2 tbsp	baking powder
500 ml (2 cups)	milk
500 ml (2 cups)	buttermilk
4	eggs, separated
1 1/2 tsp	cardamom (optional)
1	lemon, grated zest
2 tbsp	sugar
1 tsp	salt
125 ml (1/2 cup)	oil or margarine, melted

Mix flour and baking powder. Gradually add milk and buttermilk, beating constantly. Add egg yolks while beating. Add cardamom, grated lemon zest, sugar, and salt. Whip egg whites stiff but not dry, and fold into batter. Bake in special ebleskiver pan using a small amount of oil. Serve warm with sugar or icing sugar and jam. Makes 50-55 ebleskiver.

Pancakes (Pandekager)

Danish pancakes are similar to crepes but sweeter. They are flat and eaten rolled up with filling inside (typically strawberry jam). My father used to make these for dinner when we wanted something extra delicious.

350 ml (1.5 cups)	flour
2 tsp	sugar
1/4 tsp	salt
1/2	lemon, grated zest
1/2 tsp	cardamom (optional)
400 ml (1 & 2/3 cup) milk	
50 ml (1/3 cup)	beer or water
3	eggs
	margarine or butter for frying

Mix flour, sugar, salt, lemon zest, and cardamom. Gradually beat milk and beer or water into flour mixture until it forms a smooth batter. Beat eggs and add to batter. Heat a little margarine in a frying pan. Pour enough batter into pan to make a thin coating. Flip pancake when golden brown on bottom, and cook the other side. Serve with sugar or icing sugar and jam. Makes 12 pancakes.

Spice Cookies *(Brunekager)*

Brunekager are famous traditional Danish Christmas cookies. Every year I would pick these up from the Danish bakery owned by one of my second cousins.

250 ml (1 cup)	butter or margarine
250 ml (1 cup)	sugar
125 ml (1/2 cup)	corn syrup
700 ml (3 cups)	flour
250 ml (1 cup)	almonds, chopped
1 tbsp	cinnamon
2 tsp	ginger
2 tsp	ground cloves
1 tsp	baking soda

Cream butter and sugar in a large bowl. Stir in corn syrup. Combine flour, almonds, cinnamon, ginger, cloves, and baking soda in a separate bowl. With a wooden spoon, gradually stir dry ingredients into butter mixture to make a soft but not sticky dough.

Divide into 4 portions. On lightly floured surface, roll each into a 3-4 cm diameter log.

Wrap in plastic wrap and refrigerate until chilled.

Cut rolls into 1/4 cm thin slices, or roll out between sheets of wax paper and cut using cookie cutters. Place 2 cm apart on greased cookie sheet. Bake in 400F oven for 8 minutes or until golden brown. Cool on pans for 3 minutes. Remove to rack to let cool completely. Makes about 8 dozen cookies.

Klejner

Another traditional holiday treat, these are just delicious. Period. It's just not Christmas without them.

3	**eggs**
250 ml (1 cup)	**sugar**
1/2 tsp	**salt**
4 tbsp	**whipping cream**
125 ml (1/2 cup)	**butter, melted**
1 tsp	**baking powder**
750 ml (3 cups)	**flour**
1 tsp	**cardamom**
750 ml (3 cups)	**Crisco or other shortening**

Beat eggs and sugar well, add cream and melted butter, then stir in enough flour to make a dough stiff enough to roll out for cookies. Cut into diamond shapes, make a slit in the center, and pull one end through the slit.

Cook in hot Crisco until light brown. Best to cook only a few (6-8) at a time, turning with a kitchen fork or metal knitting needle. Remove and let cool on clean brown paper or strong paper towels.

Jule Gløgg

Gløgg is a delicious Scandinavian version of mulled wine perfect for cold, winter evenings. I never liked Gløgg growing up, but now it reminds me of familiar hygge moments from my childhood. I recommend serving it with the ebleskiver. Yum!

2 L (8 cups)	red wine, dry
2 L (8 cups)	apple juice
1 L (4 cups)	water
4 tbsp	orange juice, frozen
1 bottle	Gløgg mix
200 ml (3/4 cup)	almonds, slivered
400 ml (1 & 2/3 cup)	raisins

Soak raisins in a bit of red wine overnight so they can absorb the flavour. Slowly heat liquid ingredients, and add raisins. Just before serving, add almonds.

Note: If you can't find Gløgg mix, you can add 8 whole cloves, 3 whole cardamom pods, and a 5 cm piece of cinnamon bark to the liquid mixture.

Sleeping Routines

After all of that eating, surely you'll be so stuffed you'll want to go to sleep! And what is more *hyggeligt* than bundling up under piles of blankets in your softest pyjamas?

The Process of Going to Bed

Here are some excellent ways to help you relish your bedtime routine:

- String faery lights above your bed, or use a bedside lamp with low-watt lightbulbs.

- Take a hot bath or shower before you go to sleep. I recommend adding a few drops of lavender essential oil.

- Wear flannel pyjamas in the wintertime or breezy cotton pyjamas in the summertime.

- Place fresh, clean sheets onto a soft mattress. Be mindful of the texture of the linens.

- Use soft blankets and pillows.

- Place a fuzzy rug next to your bed.

- Spray your favourite soothing scents or light a scented candle. Lavender is great for putting you in a relaxed mood.

- Drink a warm cup of decaffeinated herbal tea.

- Read a good book. Fiction is less likely to over-stimulate your mind.

- Invite a furry friend—if you let them sleep in your bed, of course!

- Make a dream pillow, and place it inside your pillowcase. Dream pillows are a type of aromatherapy dating back to 16th Century Europe, where they were used to help people sleep peacefully, without nightmares or restlessness.

Dream Pillow Instructions

You'll need:

- 1/2 cup of an equal blend of dried hops, roses, chamomile, and lavender

- One 5" x 12" piece of cotton fabric (prewashed)

- Needle & thread

- Cotton batting or fibrefill

Sew your pillow with the right sides together, leaving an end open to insert herbs and cotton.

Turn right side out, place cotton on bottom of pillow.

Add herbs, and sew up the hole.

Place this inside your pillowcase, and have sweet dreams!

The Process of Waking Up

After that amazing, deep sleep you had last night, you can also enhance your morning routine. Mornings can become boring and repetitive, but embracing the *hygge* mindset can help.

- Wake up an extra half an hour early. Being able to slow down your morning and ease into the day is better on your mind and soul.

- Practice some gentle yoga stretches. Our muscles are usually stiff in the morning, so this will help you get limber and ready for the day. YouTube and mobile apps are great for getting your daily dose of yoga.

- Put on some fuzzy slippers.

- Play music that energizes you or slowly wakes you up. Check out playlists on Apple Music, Spotify, or Songza. Or make your own!

- Drink a full glass of warm water with a few slices of lemon to get your digestive system going.

- This one is important. Eat breakfast. Your body needs the fuel. I also recommend drinking a nice, hot cup of tea.

- Avoid technology, and enjoy a moment of silence without distractions.

Hygge Exercise

Hygge may be relaxing, but it doesn't mean a lack of activity—far from it! In fact, an active lifestyle is essential to staying happy and healthy. It gives us energy, boosts our immune system, controls weight gain, and promotes better sleep. It's also great for our emotional and mental wellbeing by reducing stress and anxiety, improving our mood and self confidence, keeping us mentally sharp, and helping us be more creative. What could be more *hyggeligt* than that?

Though studies have shown various results, the general consensus is that we should exercise at least 30 minutes per day.

I'm not a fitness instructor by any stretch of the imagination. In fact, I'm guilty of *not* always enjoying exercise, but I've found a few ways to stay active that I actually enjoy and are also very *hyggeligt!*

Yoga

Specifically, try Yin Yoga, which is a slower-paced style of yoga where a pose is held for five or more minutes. In this type of yoga, you allow your body to fall and fold into each position. It's especially relaxing when paired with soft music and scented candles or essential oils. But really, any type of yoga is amazing for your mind and body.

Walk

Another great way to get exercise is taking walks out in nature. The Danes love going on long walks. The weather is never an issue; just dress appropriately. If it's raining, use an umbrella, or wear rain boots and a raincoat. Take a stroll in the park or along the beach. Go for a romantic night walk. These are especially wonderful during the summertime when the evenings are still warm. End the night with a cup of hot chocolate over candlelight.

Ride Your Bike

Bicycling is a common mode of transportation in Denmark. You'll never see so many bicycles in your life as you will parked along the streets of Copenhagen. Here in Vancouver, many people use their bike to commute to and from work as well.

Riding a bike is not only good for the environment, it's phenomenal at keeping us in shape. A *hyggeligt* bike ride is a calming and relaxing one, the kind you take on a warm summer's day with nowhere to be, maybe with a friend accompanying you. You could also pack a lunch and stop at a beautiful park to rest and enjoy a picnic.

Dance with Your Partner

There's nothing more *hyggeligt* than spending quality time with your loved ones. My significant other and I recently took Lindy Hop lessons, which is a type of jazz and swing dance made popular in the late 1930s and early 1940s. Any kind of ballroom dancing is a great way to not only get a great workout but to bond with your partner.

Go on a Hike

Hiking up a mountain is a great way to get the benefits of exercise while taking in some beautiful scenery. It improves your cardio-respiratory fitness and builds your muscles. It's also great at reducing depression and helping you sleep better.

Experts say if you hike for at least two and a half hours a week, you will feel the benefits. Combine it with great company and delicious snacks, and you're all set for the ideal *hyggeligt* experience!

Run

Now, I don't personally relate to this one, but I have many friends who swear that running helps them clear their minds. So if you're the type of person who finds solace in a good, long run, this is a great way to stay in shape.

Go Outside

Try to spend more time outdoors. We can get so used to going to the gym and running on a treadmill that we miss the boost of energy we get from simply being outside and breathing in the fresh air.

Perhaps gardening is your favorite mode of relaxation. And with hardly realizing it, you can end up burning a lot of calories mowing the lawn or planting flowers. You could also embrace your nurturing side by growing your own vegetable garden and enjoying the nutritional benefits as well.

No matter what you choose to do when you exercise, it's all about making the activity fun, being present, and noticing the little details. Sometimes the smallest things give us the biggest memories.

Relationships

A *hyggeligt* relationship is respectful, honest, and kind. It's about connecting with the other person, having empathy, and being generous. It's spending time with people we care about: our friends, our families, and our significant others.

Especially during the wintertime when it gets cold and dark out, it can be tempting to want to hide away indoors. But the *hygge* mindset sees this for what it is—a great opportunity to instead reconnect with our loved ones who we may have been too busy to spend quality time with.

Why not open the doors to your home and invite someone over, even if you're not usually the hosting type? Remember, it doesn't have to be a highly planned ordeal. We don't need to cook elaborate feasts and scrub the floors and counters until we see our reflection in them.

It's more important to actually make those human connections, to practice the art of intimacy. Take the time to have deep, meaningful conversations, and find sanctuary in the company of your guests.

This means turn off the technology, and be present with the person across from you! We don't need to keep ourselves connected with social media 24/7 in order to be fulfilled. Real fulfillment is right in front of you.

Just as much as doing something familiar is comforting, you can always try to choose new activities in order to create new memories. Think outside the box, and skip the coffee date. Try the 300-flavour ice cream shop instead.

If you're ever feeling overwhelmed, you can always see people in small doses. However, while it may seem like a difficult task to get dressed, leave the house, and spend time with others, at the end of the day, you'll have a new sense of balance and happiness that you took the time to catch up with someone you hadn't seen in a long time.

Hygge Gifts!

Gift giving can be very difficult. Sometimes we just don't know what to get someone, especially when that person already has everything. But you're in luck because *hygge* is all about thrift and simplicity.

A *hyggeligt* gift is one where a lot of thought has gone into it. *Hygge* gifts come from the heart, are homemade, often DIY, and don't cost very much.

So the next time a gift-giving event comes around, try not to buy a gift just for the sake of buying something. It's not fair for either the giver or the receiver. Instead, really get creative, and choose something with a personal touch. You'll find that the possibilities are endless!

The Gift of Time

Sometimes we get so caught up in our to-do lists that we forget to spend time with those we love. Why not cook dinner for a friend, or offer to babysit their children so they can go on a date? Perhaps you could weed your grandmother's garden that needs some tending to, or offer your talents, such as photography, financial planning, or hairstyling.

Gift Experiences

If you're having trouble thinking of a gift for someone who has a lot of things, try giving them a new experience instead. Concerts, sports games, or plays are always an entertaining option. Or you could gift a weekend getaway at a spa resort or ski mountain.

The activities don't have to be extravagant. You could gift a ticket to a local attraction, such as a museum, or dinner for two at their favourite restaurant. Or the gift of new skills, such as pottery or guitar classes, could end up introducing them to their new favorite hobby.

Charity

Try donating in their name to a cause that is related to something that they care about. For example, the S.P.C.A. for the animal lover, a local film festival for the arts lover, or the International Red Cross for the humanitarian.

DIY

If you're going to give something that is tangible, a *hyggeligt* option is definitely something homemade. If you scour the pages of Pinterest, you will never be without options, whether it's mixing your own sugar scrub, making a terrarium, painting a mug, or building a bookshelf. DIY candles are also very easy to make—the gift of *hygge*!

Sentimental Gifts

Heirlooms make wonderful gifts for that special family member. She'll love that piece of jewellery that was  originally owned by your great great grandmother, and he'll appreciate that original gramophone player that has been passed down since the early 1900s.

A sentimental gift can also be an item that is meaningful to the recipient, such as a gift that reminds them of a special memory. This could be a framed photograph of your trip to Italy together or really anything the two of you share.

Wrapping

A *hyggeligt* way to wrap gifts is with classic, brown paper, wrapped in twine or string with some piece of nature, such as an evergreen branch or a dried flower. My aunts in Denmark always sent me packages wrapped like this.

The best thing is, you never have to go out and buy wrapping paper. If you're looking to have something for a specific occasion, dress up the paper with your own drawings in a black Sharpie.

Cards

Instead of spending $5-$10 on a card, just make your own. There are plenty of possibilities, like drawing your own artwork or pasting scrapbooking pieces onto the card. Spend some time writing a meaningful note inside as well.

If cards aren't your thing, write a handwritten letter or start a card journal for those you know you'll always be celebrating with, such as your spouse or children.

Instead of spending money on a new card every birthday, anniversary, or holiday, just to have it thrown out, dedicate a journal to that person, and write or draw your message inside for them to hold onto forever. Not only is this economical, it's also sentimental and amazing to flip through again and again.

Endless Hygge Possibilities

The possibilities are endless when it comes to *hygge*. Below is a list of even more ways to incorporate some *hygge* into your life. Remember, *hyggeligt* activities are simple, old fashioned, and about bringing joy to everyday routines. If we manage to enjoy all the little things, we will be able to look back and realize that they were also the big things.

- Explore *hyggeligt* places outside your home, such as cities, parks, pubs, and coffee shops.

- Have a bonfire. Invite the neighbours, and serve hot apple cider.

- Plan an intimate, candlelit dinner with friends.

- Take a warm, silky bath. Add scented candles and relaxing tunes.

- Bake your own fresh bread. Savour the smells!

- Watch a movie with your family.

- At Christmas, decorate the home with your family. Make your own decorations, such as traditional Danish paper mobiles. Drink Jule Gløgg, and eat sweets.

- Catch a sunset or sunrise.

- Visit the bird sanctuary.

- Hang a calendar.

- Snuggle under the blanket when it snows.

- Pick berries or nuts in the countryside.

- Have a picnic in the park with a loved one.

- Read a good book. Read physical books instead of eBooks.

- Relax by the fire.

- Read bedtime stories to your child.

- Go for afternoon tea.

- Enjoy a cup of coffee in a cozy café.

- Go to a concert.

- Take photos with a film camera.

- Take walks in the snow at night.

- Make a blanket fort.

- Walk the dog.

- Learn something new by taking low-key classes, such as pottery or other crafts with some friends.

- Use flannel sheets!

- Light candles instead of using lamps.

- Make a list of everything that makes you happy.

- Turn off technology.

- Play board games or card games.

- Sing. Singing is a very *hyggeligt* Danish pastime.

- Colour in a cozy restaurant with your child.

- Learn to knit or sew.

- Make handmade invitations and greeting cards.

- Write handwritten letters, and mail them.

- Keep a physical address book.

- Keep a journal.

- Print pictures, and make photo albums.

- Start a book club.

- Run errands with your best friend.

- Rent a cabin with friends.

- Fly a kite.

- Plan an outdoor summer picnic with friends during sunset on a warm, summer evening.

- Volunteer at an animal shelter or seniors' home.

- Enjoy a glass of wine.

- Do some yard work.

- Dry fresh flowers.

- Pick wildflowers, and put them in a vase at home.

Have more activities to add? Jot them down below.

_____

_____

_____

_____

_____

_____

_____

_____

Adding more *hygge* to your everyday life will certainly bring you much joy. As you can see, you can incorporate *hygge* into pretty much any area of your life, whether it's in your home, the way you exercise, or how you interact with others.

PART 4:
Hygge and
Wellbeing

Hygge and Wellbeing

In this final chapter, we'll go through all of the benefits that *hygge* has on our wellbeing. Though the possibilities are tremendous and diverse, there are certain specific ingredients to creating a more fulfilling life, such as focusing on what is important.

Living a simpler, present, and focused life helps us add purpose to who we are and what we want to accomplish. It makes us happier people and strengthens our relationships.

The Busyness Illusion

As technology advances in our modern world, we find ourselves living in a society that moves faster than ever before. We are constantly connected via Wi-Fi or cellular network and check our email and social media accounts frequently.

We can have everything at our fingertips: an email sent from the other side of the world, a movie streamed instantly, money transferred online, a customized music channel, even a date with someone who shares our interests.

Ironically, while we are more connected than we have ever been, and convenience is at an all-time high, we have grown distracted and disconnected from ourselves. We rarely have a moment to contemplate who we are because we are struggling with information overload. The hours slip by right before our eyes, and we suffer from a loss of personal authenticity.

For those of us who live in the city, we find ourselves always rushing from one place to another, eating on the go, catching transit, and running around between errands. It's a constant rat race, as we try to make more money so we can afford more things, and then make even more money to be able to keep up with monthly payments and the expectations of our lifestyle.

It's easy to feel this pressure; however, such rampant consumerism is not sustainable. We will eventually find ourselves exhausted and feeling like something is missing.

This sort of lifestyle also disconnects us from our true internal creativity and motivation. This system breeds a way of life where our outer actions, experiences, or material possessions are a measurement of how we compare to our peers. In doing so, this competitive way of life devalues our inner honesty and integrity, making us only as good as the image we portray.

The joy in the simple things, such as making a home-cooked meal, cleaning the house, planting our own herbs, or inviting someone over for tea has been removed because we perceive them as difficult and time-consuming. We need to pause once in a while, embrace the calm, and find joy in the small details, even in the tasks that seem so mundane.

Children today are growing up in this culture of busyness, thinking that it is a normal way of being, and they aren't given the time to themselves and their imaginations. If we live in a society where only accomplishment and outer appearances are important, what does this teach our future generations? If children are taught that only results matter, we take away the creative process necessary to build a child's true passions and identities. Filling a child's day with piano, swimming, soccer, and dance lessons is great, but they should be given equal time to be alone and discover who they are without external influences.

Hygge is a practical way to counteract an overly stuffed lifestyle. By applying the concept of *hygge* in our everyday lives, we can learn to be more intentional about being more present and savouring the moment. Having the ability to just *be* is more than we can ever ask for, and it gives us real joy. *Hygge* is a practical way to find and strengthen deeper connections to our loved ones, our homes, our planet, and ourselves.

> *"You will never be free until you have no need to impress anyone."*

Hyggeligt Minimalism

The opposite of a *hygge* lifestyle is one of excess. Because *hygge* is about *being*, not having, it instead encourages thriftiness, frugality, and non-consumerism. *Hygge* is about real togetherness with our families and loved ones.

When we are not focused on buying the next best thing, we focus on real, down-to-earth relationships. The safety we believe we get from owning nice things is an illusion. *Hygge* is accessible to anyone no matter where we are on the social ladder.

In our culture we are taught that the more we have, the happier we will be. Thanks to rampant advertisement, we are conditioned to believe that life is about owning a bigger house, a nicer car, and wearing high-end brands.

As a society, we need to question these social constructs. Studies show time and time again that, while having a lot of money may buy us "security," it doesn't necessarily make us any happier. Without love or real connection, we are left feeling empty inside.

Whether or not this way of life is for you, I think we can all agree that being more mindful and intentional about our choices will improve our quality of life. Every aspect of ourselves can be whittled down to the essentials.

So, what is Minimalism?

Minimalism means getting rid of excess distractions so we can focus on what is important. By simplifying our lives, we are able to think more clearly, be less stressed, and have more time for the things that really matter to us.

Minimalism is about living intentionally, mindfully, and consciously. It's also about keeping our priorities in line with our values and who we want to be.

Hyggeligt minimalism takes this one step further. It's about surrounding yourself with things that you love and  not excess clutter that serves no purpose. Every item is studied to see if it enhances your life. When you look around your home, you want to feel joy, comfort, love, and perhaps a little nostalgia for those sentimental items as well.

With *hyggeligt* minimalism, we can create a world around us that is safe, joyful, and stress free. We listen to that little voice inside ourselves to guide us. We trust and are confident in ourselves because even if we lose everything we've got, we are still a valuable human being. We are not what we own.

It can be easy in life to fall into the trap of comparing ourselves to others based on their success and material possessions. Life is not about that. When it's all over, we'll look back at our lives and hope we lived meaningfully, gave back, inspired people, focused on our passions, connected with friends and family, and didn't stress over having the latest and greatest.

True happiness cannot be found externally; it must be found from within. And when we do, we become centered, connected, and unshakable.

Apply Hyggeligt Minimalism to All Areas of Your Life

Here are a few key areas to focus on when decluttering:

- Time commitments: Only say *yes* to things that bring you value.

- Finances: Make an effort to spend less money on things.

- Our digital self: Clear out excess files, unsubscribe from junk mail, and spend less time surfing the Internet.

- Clothing: Only keep what you love and wear.

- Food: Choose to eat healthy, whole foods only, reducing or eliminating caffeine, alcohol, sugar, and processed foods.

- Negative self-talk: Learn to control your thoughts, and only allow positivity in.

- Distractions/vices: Get rid of any habit that is not good for you.

- People: Cut your ties from those who are negative to be around, and surround yourself with those who lift you.

A book I always recommend is Marie Kondo's *The Life Changing Magic of Tidying Up* if you want to go deep into the decluttering process. The Kon Mari Method is a cleaning technique where you only keep things that "spark joy" when you hold the item in your hands.

Marie anthropomorphizes objects, teaching you to show them love and appreciation and to thank them for their purpose. For example, if there are gifts or cards you don't want to keep but feel guilty about getting rid of, know that the purpose of a gift/card is to convey someone's emotions about you. Once that purpose has been served, you have no other obligation to keep the item.

The benefits are endless! When we give ourselves more space, we notice a huge shift. I promise you, it's one of those things that you can't really understand until you try it. The lightness that occurs is freeing. The idea that we can let go of constantly *wanting* things is so liberating, you'll never go back. Say hello to:

- Less stuff to clean (yay!)

- Less stress

- Saving more money – goodbye to financial strains!

- Worrying about our possessions – they don't own us

- More freedom

- Less consumption and more care for the environment

- Less focus on the superficial

- More confidence

- Less fear of failure

- Owning high-quality things

- More happiness!

- More time to focus on health, loved ones, and our passions

- No more keeping up with the Joneses

- Being more present

- Inner peace and a centered state of mind

"We buy things we don't need with money we don't have to impress people we don't like."
~ Dave Ramsey

Being Okay with Solitude

It's extremely important to spend time alone with ourselves in order to dream and reflect. When we can become comfortable with introspection and idleness, we find the space to figure out who we really are.

It's a very Danish thing to pause and allow the previous day, week, or month to catch up with us. It's about finding our inner sanctuary and comforting ourselves.

Jeppe Trolle Linnet talks about the state of *hvile i sig selv* (resting in oneself). "It is often mentioned by Danes as a highly attractive personal trait. It is viewed as the unassailable condition of people who have supposedly arrived at the point where they mainly care about living up to their own standards and not those of others...he is happy. Exuding an air of calm, self-assured balance is therefore crucial for sending off cultural signs by which one is seen as a cool, stylish, and graceful human being," he says.

In order to do this, try to find some time where you can relax and be undisturbed. Don't be tempted to surf your mobile device or turn on the television.

Instead, take yourself out on a day date to your favourite museum, or make some crafts. You could also just make your favourite cup of tea or go for a scenic bike ride. Allow your soul to catch up to your body, and don't feel the need to distract yourself.

Some of us don't have much time for solitude. Maybe we work with people all week and then come home to a house full of more people. While connecting with people is a wonderful thing, it's more important to be able to connect with ourselves.

Solitude allows us to develop our natural ability to build our inner creativity. Being constantly busy actually hampers our imagination, while boredom and idleness actually help invite inspiration, despite what society may tell us.

We are taught that we should always be productive, keep busy, join clubs, and so on, but if we are always focused on achieving things, when do we get to spend time doing what comes innately from our souls?

When we're bored, we're forced to come up with creative solutions to entertain ourselves, and this is good for the mind. It makes us draw, write, build, engineer, and create.

We're so used to shielding our uncomfortable feelings of boredom with external distractions like television, internet, or perhaps stronger vices, such as drinking, drugs, and partying. But we don't actually need to always be stimulated in order to be happy—quite the opposite, in fact!

When was the last time you took a moment to reflect? Perhaps this already is your natural way of being, or perhaps this is something you'd love to get better at. But the truth is we can't really understand others if we don't take the time to understand ourselves. That effort may be a bit uncomfortable at first, but push through it! If you take it head-on and don't try to cover it up, it will get easier.

Try meditation. You can start small, such as 5 minutes a day, and gradually increase it to 20 minutes a day as you get into it. Meditation benefits us mentally, physically, and emotionally.

Studies have shown that meditation increases our overall happiness, wellbeing, and health. It lowers high blood pressure, decreases pain, improves the immune system, and boosts energy. It also centers us and leaves us at a calmer base state. It reduces stress, stimulates creativity, makes us feel more connected to others and ourselves, improves brain function, and helps us sleep better. Who wouldn't want any of those things?

Hygge and Our Inner Child

One of the most life-changing things that *hygge* has done for me is reconnecting me with my inner child. Truth be told, I don't think I would have written this book without it.

I was at my parents' house one day in the countryside, looking through my old childhood toys, schoolwork, and art, and I came across a pile of fifty-odd books I had written when I was between the ages of 5 and 10.

I grew up as an only child, so I learned how to enjoy my own company without relying on others to entertain me. Because I spent a lot of time alone, it sparked my creativity, and I was always creating new things: writing books, making up songs, creating art, and so on.

Lately I had been asking myself the question, *What did I love doing when I was younger?* And I realized before society had time to influence how I should spend my time, I'd spend it writing books. Instead of fiction, they were more of the activity, science, art, and research type books, similar to this one. I decided right then that I'd rekindle that inner fire and try writing again as an adult, and it feels amazing!

Some of us are lucky to know what we loved doing right from the start and have continued to master our craft ever since. But some of us lose sight somewhere along our journey and have to reconnect with our natural passions later on. Unfortunately, some of us get caught up with the busyness of life and never make that reconnection.

Now, I'm not saying this is necessary; some feel a strong need to move away from childhood things. But if you ever find yourself wondering if there's something else out there, consider checking back in with yourself and reflecting on what used to make you happy. I find that tapping into what you loved as a child can bring a *hyggeligt* sense of purpose and authenticity. You might even regain a kind of joy that was long forgotten.

If you have children of your own, don't forget to give them space to reconnect, reflect, explore and be creative. Playtime is essential for a developing human being. It's normal for parents to want the best for their child, however, studies say that it is more important not to overwhelm them with endless activities or an abundance of toys as they are unable to process or rationalize all of the information. Ultimately, it's more beneficial to provide children with a calm, *hyggeligt,* and simple environment so they can really thrive.

What were some activities you loved doing as a child when nobody told you had to do them? Write them in the space below.

_____

_____

_____

_____

"Can you remember who you were
before the world told you
who to be?"
~ Danielle LaPorte

How Hygge Can Help You with the Winter Blues

For many of us, winter is associated with sleeping as much possible, avoiding social events, and feeling dull in general. Ironically, while a part of us only wants to rest and do absolutely nothing, we also get so swept up in the holiday festivities that we end up with a surplus of obligations (and a few extra pounds). Before we know it, we can end up feeling exhausted and drained.

Some of us are also sensitive to the changes of the weather. Seasonal Affective Disorder (SAD) is a type of depression that usually occurs during autumn and winter when there is a lack of sunlight. SAD affects half a million people every winter between September and April with the worst span being from December to February. Symptoms include depression, anxiety, apathy, mood changes, sleep problems, lethargy, overeating, undereating, sexual problems, and no desire to socialize.

The winter blues is a milder form of SAD.

When I was a child, I suffered from a strong case of the winter blues. I wouldn't eat, I was constantly crying, and my doctor told me that if I didn't try to get better, I'd have to sit in front of a therapy lamp.

The so-called "happy lamp" is one traditional form of treatment. Used every morning to trick the body that the sun was rising, this would suppress excessive melatonin production, a major contributor to SAD. It seems to have significant positive impact on users.

We can also spend more time outdoors and get more natural sunlight exposure. If nothing else works, one can take antidepressants to reduce the extreme feelings of despair and hopelessness in the winter months. But those come with their own list of side effects.

*Note that I am not a therapist, and if you are dealing with severe depression, please consult a doctor or psychologist.

So how can *hygge* help with SAD? Remember that a *hyggeligt* life is about seeking and keeping a positive mindset. *Hygge* is about making peace with the cold, dark, and wet winters and is a joyful, warm, and cozy way to cope with the blues.

Dealing with constant darkness is difficult for even the happiest people, but in Denmark, they have *hygge* to look forward to. It helps people reframe the wintertime into a very positive event. And likewise, learning to embrace the cold weather helps your body's natural circadian rhythm adjust to the darker, shorter days during wintertime. You ease yourself into the season and suffer much less.

Try not to isolate yourself, no matter how much you feel like shutting the world out. It may be difficult to take that first step towards getting dressed, but you'll be glad when you feel that warmth of having connected with another human being.

Hygge and Gratitude

Gratitude is an emotion focused on appreciating what you have, rather than always wanting more. It's the quality of being thankful and returning that kindness to others, and it's a central component of *hygge*.

If we can cultivate more gratitude, we will increase our happiness and general wellbeing. Studies also find that it is associated with increased energy, optimism, and empathy, and it helps us deal with stress, anxiety, and fear.

It's just like starting a new exercise routine—you have to make the conscious decision to build and maintain that habit. For example, keep a gratitude journal, even if it's just a note on your mobile phone. Or start a gratitude jar, filling it up with things you are grateful for. Write down things that you are grateful for every day.

Then take this a step further, and give back to others, whether it's volunteering for a cause or helping a friend or family member. Give compliments.

As soon as you find yourself thinking negatively or criticizing something, switch the thought to a positive one immediately. Everything we think will be downloaded into our subconscious minds, so it's important to fill ourselves with positivity.

Don't get wrapped up in someone else's misery. For example, when they whine and complain about the cold, change the subject or at least the focus of the conversation. Talk about how it's a great opportunity to bundle up in blankets and drink tea, go skiing, or make snow angels. Life will be much more joyful.

A Final Note

By now you should have a pretty good idea of how to add more *hygge* to your life. You have learned about the history of *hygge,* what it means to *hygge,* and ways to make every moment more special. I hope that, through it all, you've found some inspiration.

Hygge has significant benefits to our everyday lives. It will improve your relationships, it's good for your mental and emotional wellbeing, and it helps you get focused on what's really important to YOU!

Thank you for picking up this book and taking the time to read it. I hope you found as much value in the *hygge* lifestyle as I did, and I hope it helped you find meaning, authenticity, love, passion, connection, and joy.

And remember...

Slow down, and enjoy life's cozy moments!

30-Day Hygge Challenge:

1	2	3	4	5
take a hot bath	watch the sunrise	reconnect with an old friend	watch a movie and relax	spend the day by yourself; enjoy the solitude
6	**7**	**8**	**9**	**10**
do something you loved as a child	find a cozy café, and enjoy a hot beverage	pick up a book you've been meaning to read	relax by the fire (or candlelight)	make a list of things that make you happy
11	**12**	**13**	**14**	**15**
stay offline for the day	plan a dinner with friends	invite someone over for tea and cookies	meditate for fifteen minutes	leave your schedule open today
16	**17**	**18**	**19**	**20**
wear fuzzy slippers	go for a walk in your comfiest outfit	write a letter to someone you miss	bake something new	cook a homemade meal
21	**22**	**23**	**24**	**25**
light a scented candle	give yourself a facial	catch a sunset	declutter your digital life	take a yoga class
26	**27**	**28**	**29**	**30**
make a homemade gift for a loved one	pick wildflowers, and put them in a vase	listen to soothing music	hug your pet or loved one	write out your dreams in a journal

About the Author

Pia Edberg is a writer, artist, and entrepreneur. With a passion for human nature, she has spent the last 15 years studying personal development and has worked in Human Resources for the past ten years. Pia wants to dedicate her life to sharing what she's learned while inspiring others through her work.

When she's not writing, she's probably wandering around an old vintage shop, playing the guitar, taking a yoga or dance class, or playing with her two adorable cats! Pia was born in Nykøbing Falster, Denmark and currently lives in beautiful Vancouver, British Columbia, Canada.

To learn more, visit www.piaedberg.com

Thank you for reading my book!

I really appreciate all of your feedback and love hearing what you have to say.

I need your input to make the next version even better.

Please leave me a helpful REVIEW on Amazon.

Thank you so much!

<3 Pia

Made in the USA
Lexington, KY
16 July 2016